Copyright

Lady Liuwa is a fictional book. The story is based on past decade wildlife crisis in Africa and local events. The name Lady Liuwa was given by the regional people to the last-living lioness in Zambia Liuwa Plain. However, the author has embellished the characters and incidents by her imagination.

To my mother, a courageous woman!

Contents

Introduction

She is alone. She hasn't seen a relative or another of her kind since her adolescence. Loneliness is her constant companion from sunrise to sunset, day in and day out, and year after year. Through the vast savannah, she rambles aimlessly—or she wanders in search of a mate. Whichever it is, time is running out. Now, she is about to pass her prime; will she find a mate? SHE IS DESPERATE FOR COMPANIONSHIP!

In Zambia, Africa, only one lioness is left roaming Zambia's vast Liuwa Plain: her pride and other lions were wiped out by humans and by lack of food stock. She has been alone for nearly eight years. Until one day while patrolling she catches sight of a vehicle parked on the grassland with a cameraman and his crew inside. Her curiosity prompts her to get close to watch these humans. Although the memory of how humans slaughtered her pride is vivid, a longing for companionship drives her to take a chance. Will she be harmed by these men, condemned to the same fate as her pride—or will her destiny be other, indulging her life with privileges and a new hope?

Liuwa Plain is in western Zambia near the border of Angola. It's a wild, remote place with a vast-open grassland and woodland. An ideal climate and fertile soil make this land a paradise for herbivores. And it is known as the home of Africa's second largest wildebeest migration after the Serengeti annual migration. In the past, hundreds of thousands of big game galloped across the plains to form a spectacular view. The migration route starts from eastern Angola across the Liuwa Plain grasslands and into the woodlands before returning to Angola.

Prior to the1970, this land was a land of plenty. As human population growths and urbanization expands, conflicts between humans and animals are intensified. Both subsistence hunting and commercial poaching threaten wildlife population. When it's man vs animal, man always wins. The wildlife population in the Liuwa Plain and in other parts of Africa dwindled rapidly. Species which have been present in large numbers before are now either extinct or rarely seen.

To aggravate the situation in the late 1990s, as the Angolan War waged on, soldiers and villagers slaughtered Liuwa's wildlife—predators as well as prey—for food. Animals once plentiful on the plains disappeared: wildebeest, buffalo, eland—all are gone. Oh, there were—how shall I say it?—glorious trophy hunters; their preference for male lions upset the pride's balance and put them in danger. Consequently, there was a shortage of prey, and trophy hunting drove the once thriving lion population to disintegrate. Sadly, the last of Liuwa's majestic alpha lion—head of a pride—became a lifeless decoration in the home of a trophy hunter.

African nations were aware of the crisis. To salvage the badly beaten ecosystem and restore wildlife population, the African Parks Network (APN) was formed. The African Parks Zambia (APZ), one of the entities in APN, is responsible for the management of the Liuwa Plain Nation Park.

When The African Parks Zambia (APZ) started their rehabilitation program in Liuwa in 2003, they succeeded in securing the Liuwa area from illegal poaching and exploitation through the park's system. All wildlife species have prospered under this protection. Slowly wildebeest and zebra herds thundered back to their renewed spectacle in the Liuwa Plain.

What about the lions? Only one lioness remains. Lions are animated by their instincts of finding mates, having cubs, and forming pride, yet, without another lion around for hundreds of miles, Lady Liuwa is deprived. How did she survive without the provision of a lion pride? Lions hunt in group; without a partner hunting is fraught with difficulties. What about emotional needs? A pride is not merely a killing machine but the heart of lions' social life, the backbone of nurturing support. Lady Liuwa's pride is gone. She has nobody. This is truly unbearable for a relationship seeking cat.

The Pride

Pride is a curious word. Pride, when most people hear this word what do they think of—a job well done, self esteem or, on the negative side, arrogance? How many people have the reflex to think of lions? Lions are the only social cats that live in groups known as prides. A pride of lions is a family structure, which may include up to three males, a dozen or so females, and, of course, their cubs aging from 0 to three years. A pride headed by one male is vulnerable to attacks by male lions outside the pride and by other predators. Two or more males in a pride will be more successful in warding off any takeover attempts by challenging males. A pride with more than one male is the best situation for long-term survival.

All of the females in a pride will be related to one another. As a rule the males of the pride are the fathers of the cubs. Female cubs often stay within the group after they have matured. Although, some young females do leave the pride as the young males do. Young males eventually leave to establish their own prides by meeting other females outside the old pride's territory or by taking over a group headed by another male. When the young males have two or three brothers, they will often leave together forming a coalition. Thus a pride can be formed with several males.

In a takeover attempt there can be several different types of tactic from posturing to a physical fight. The least violent form is a sort of posturing in which two males sit a few feet apart, face-to-face, and stare at each other. The first one to break his stare is the loser. The more violent confrontation in the pride power-control struggle ends in a physical fight. Occasionally, the fight leads to death. Surviving losers often become nomads. It is interesting to note that there can be a takeover fight between two males within a pride. Since there can be only one alpha male in a pride who has the power and authority, all other males are his subjects along with the lionesses and cubs. More often than not a subject male will launch an attack to challenge the alpha male if he perceives him to be weak and unworthy to lead. When a takeover occurs the defeated—the old alpha male—gets to stay in the pride and eat and enjoy the pride's protection (a lion's version of human retirement).

Only male lions can boast of their manes. The young male has a short-blond mane encircling the head; the mature male has a mane with dark color that covers the backside of the head and the shoulders. The scale of the mane varies from individual to individual—with some having no mane at all, while others have a sumptuous mane that runs along the body to the abdomen. It is interesting to note that lionesses prefer dark-mane lions.

The cubs are sired by the alpha male. Does he allow other males to mate with his lionesses? That will depend on the individual, alpha male. Males defend the pride's territory, which may include some ten square miles. Their duties in defending the land are: patrolling their turf by marking the area with urine, roaring menacingly to warn intruders, and chasing off animals that encroach on their land.

Lions rub each other in greeting; they lick each other while grooming. Rubbing and licking enhance their bonding. There are scent glands on the corners of their mouth. The scent will be deposited on the other lions during rubbing and licking. In addition, male lions will spray other lions as a means of bond strengthening.

In a pride, the females do most of the hunting. Although the males can hunt and do make a formidable hunter with their size, power, and strength, they rely on the females to provide them with food. At the dinner table a social hierarchy is observed. The alpha male eats first, and then the other males along with the females. The cubs are the last ones to eat. Sometimes an alpha male will allow cubs to eat with him. If there is an outcast of the pride the outcast must wait till everyone has eaten. Usually there are only scraps left for them to eat.

****

In a remote area in the Liuwa Plain resides a pride of lions: two males, four females, five young. The two males are brothers who have left their old pride and have wandered off together in search of a new territory.

They came upon several lionesses during their exploration. The first encounter was a lone female. Gently and gallantly, they padded up to the lioness, greeting her with a low moan, and waving their luxurious manes. *"Hello, Lady, can we join you in your walk?"* proposed the brothers. She only glanced at them and bounced away. No luck, she didn't even turn her head.

On account of the previous rejection they needed courage when another lioness stepped into their view. The brave brother, excitedly, advanced towards the lioness with pluck, while the other was trailing behind to avoid another embarrassment. *"Hello, Lady, can we join you in your walk?"*

"Back off, you are intruding in my territory," growled the lioness fiercely, with her paws swatting the air ready to attack. She had cubs hidden in the bush. She was going to protect them with all her might. The males sprang back as quickly as they could. They didn't want any trouble.

The third try worked like a charm. Two lionesses were in their lie-up grooming, they saw two males approaching. They got up to their feet and exclaimed to each other, *"We have visitors!"*

Each lioness looked the other one over, *"How's my tail? Is my nose clean?"*

"You have a hyena hair behind your ear."

"Oh, no, get that off me!"

Each one touched up the other to look their best. Their spirits were boosted, their faces were beaming. They were eager to meet some new friends.

Seeing two beautiful lionesses with a friendly attitude was very encouraging to the males. Even the shy brother plucked up his courage. So both strolled up, gazing softly upon their lionesses.

"Hello, Ladies, can we join you in your walk?" addressed a deep voice that captured the hearts of our lionesses.

"Most certainly, where do you come from and what are you doing here?" asked the lionesses curiously.

The males stood before them with the wind running through their manes. One spoke up shaking his mane, *"Well, if you do want to know, we are scouting out a new territory."*

With a wink the lionesses replied, *"We know where to go."*

The four hit it off. They spent hours relating their stories. The thrilled females led them to a better location with more game and more hiding spots. Together they kept on journeying till they found a well-chosen place for their new home.

When they were settling down in their new found land, two other lionesses appeared. The two males were enchanted by their presence, and the two other females were as generous as one could be. The rubbing and licking that ensued signaled their acceptance of each other. A formidable pride was born.

As soon as they had settled down, two sets of litters came —four cubs were born from one lioness followed by three cubs from another. Unfortunately, each mother lost one cub at birth. The survivors were one female and two males from one mother and two females from another. Shortly after the third lioness got pregnant and gave birth to two litters. Sadly, both died within a few days.

Here comes the problem. Two nursing lionesses with a total of five cubs demands an extra supply of food. Yet, this is a lean time because of the Angolan War. Big game is dwindling rapidly. Humans are hunting the same game for food. At the dinner table lions squabbling for food becomes nasty. More often than not they all have to go away still hungry.

During this difficult time the male lions take part in providing food whenever there is an opportunity. One day while patrolling together, they spot a lone eland head down grazing. "Brother, let's go and jump on it!" In a frenetic struggle a kill is made.

"Wuh-ooow, wuh-ooow. Come here to eat." the males call to the pride.

The lionesses hear the call from the field. Hastily they stash the cubs in a bush and scurry to the kill. They are elated to see a large prize. Something they haven't tasted for a long time.

"Oh, I need this food to nurse!" utter the two lioness mothers in unison. They gorge and gorge, continuing to feed on the carcass after the males and the two other lionesses have finished eating.

Licking their lips satisfied with their meal, there is still some meat left. The alpha male straddles his front legs over the remains. He drags it to a shady spot and covers it with leaves and branches. He will guard this carcass for the pride to eat later.

Following a big meal it's time for grooming and nursing. Inside the den there is a jumble of paws, heads, and tails as the pride huddles together. Two lionesses without cubs lick each other affectionately. The cubs are suckling. To get more milk out of mom's teats, the cubs press their paws on mom's breast. If the cubs are not satisfied with mom's milk, they can suckle from another nursing lioness.

With their tummies filled, the cubs start to play. Some are chasing each other; others are flipping summersault on mom's back. One cub finds it interesting to pounce on the male lion's twitching tail; another is biting his mane. After putting up enough with their nonsense, the male stands up, stretches, and walks away. All the playfulness serves one purpose—to enhance family bonding.

Unfortunately, this snap shot of a happy family picture is flawed. The cubs are thin. The adults look pale. There is not enough food going around for everyone; they often go hungry. Because of lack of sufficient milk, weak cubs become sick and eventually die. Pretty soon, only three adolescent cubs survive—two females from one mother and one male from their aunt.

The two lionesses without cubs forged a closer relationship with each other setting them apart from the rest of the pride. Frustrated by the squabbling and scrambling for food at the dinner table, they decide to leave the pride in search of a better life else where. It is common for pride members to leave and return, but this time these two are gone forever.

The sole male cub is full of nerve and mischief. Even though a few months younger than his cousins, he is a self-appointed leader in play time. Nothing pleases him more than ambushing his cousins. *"Here they come."* The naughty cub darts behind a cover, crouches down, and waits for the two female cubs to pass. *Onslaught!* He leaps out and lands on one of the females. To revenge themselves, the girls chase him down. One bites his tail; another knocks him down. Flipped on his back, four paws fluttering in air, the boy begs for mercy. No such luck! The two sisters take advantage of the situation and vent out their accumulated gripes by smacking their cousin's upturned belly.

The mischievous boy doesn't just get in trouble with his cousins, he often finds himself being disciplined by the adults. One time he led his cousins to the riverbank to play when the adults were out hunting. The cubs were told not to go to the riverbank to drink by themselves, for the riverbank was filled with dangerous crocodiles. While the cubs were playing boisterously on the riverbank, one giant crocodile emerged and was crawling towards the cubs. In the nick of time, one lioness returned from hunting. Seeing the danger, she immediately lunged at the crocodile. In a flash, the crocodile splashed back into the river.

Turning to the cubs, the lioness stares sternly into each one's eyes and interrogates, *"Who was the leader of this game? Didn't we tell you not to come to the riverbank by yourselves? Do you know the river is filled with cub-eating crocodiles waiting underneath the water to assault unwary lion cubs?"*

Frightened, the girls, hurriedly, sputter out, *"Our cousin led us to the riverbank. He said he had a secret to show us."*

11

"No, I didn't," denies the boy flatly, *"the girls wanted me to show them my secret. They followed me voluntarily."*

"I suppose your secret is the crocodile, my boy," the lioness sighs with anguish on her face. The distressed mother can't help fearing the worst if the male cub should step out of the line again. She asks her sister to spank the kid. *"Sister, your boy deserves a reprimand for the fright he caused us. He has to learn what is dangerous and to stay away from harm's way before it's too late."*

Jointly the two lionesses growl at the male adolescent and corner him. Submissively he rolls on his back to receive the blows on his belly from lionesses' paws. Remarkably, the pride members understand and accept the disciplines from higher ranking members through their instincts.

The Tragedy

Dinner time is another trouble time for our male adolescent. He has one insatiable appetite. He often gets whacked by the adult males for eating too much. *"Mom, dad and uncle are mean to me, they won't let me eat,"* he complains to the lioness.

"Son, game is scarce nowadays. We are rationing food. Don't you think we all want to feast on a fat kill?" replies mom with a long sigh.

"Yes, mom, we all want to feast on a fat kill, and we all can feast on a fat kill," utters the boy with a glint in his eyes. He is thinking of the livestock he spotted while roaming through the human settlement. He suggests to mom to sneak into the animal enclosure at night. At first mom rejects the idea for fear of man's retaliation. Later she succumbs to her son's repeated pleading, *"Mom, you can do it, you can do it. Mom I'm hungry, and dad won't let me eat...."*

A half-moon glows on the plains, the nocturnal carnivores, a mother lioness and her cub, tiptoe to the outskirts of a boma. One can hear *"Moo, moo—"* coming from inside the boma. The livestock is embracing a day's rest. Some are dozing off. When the day is about to end just like any other day, a thunder like roaring pierces the enclosure. The startled livestock look up, and are frightened by what they see. Two lions growl fiercely and plunge at the calf. The calf is taken down. Screams and howls erupt from the livestock.

Upon hearing the noise, the farmer rushes out with his rifle. *Boom, boom.* The mother lioness is shot at the heart and drops to the ground; the cub is shot at the rump and runs away. The farmer feels lucky that the beasts didn't get his livestock.

Covered with blood, the cub is back at the lions' den. He is panting and his heart is almost jumping out of his mouth. The pride members quickly surround him to show support and to lick his wound in an attempt to heal it. Unfortunately, the cub looses his battle with his fate. He dies in the midst of his loving pride members.

Everyone is saddened by the tragedy. The pride members mourn over the body. Where is the mom? The absence of the cub's mom casts a chilly shadow. They can only expect the worse.

In this den which is the last lion holdout a pride of eleven is reduced to four. An adult male and a female and two young lionesses are gorging in frenzy their meal—a warthog. They haven't eaten for two weeks. Food is scarce; what is also true is that there are less and less mouths to feed. Where did those uncles, aunts, and cousins go?

While crunching on a bone the alpha male lion thinks of his brother. He remembers the last time when they were patrolling together. *Boom, boom*, this sound haunts his memory. In a flashback, he can see his brother jerking then dropping to the ground. He remembers when he looked up and saw a man standing a few yards away, pointing his riffle at them. *Buzz*, a bullet hissed by his ear. He barely escaped the bullet. Horrified, the alpha male spun around and ran for his life.

After the meal the alpha lion sets out patrolling to mark the territory (about ten miles in radius). He is alone; his brother is no longer there. He leaves his scent—urine—in the grass, in the dirt, and on the tree barks to warn against any potential intruder. Doggedly he keeps on patrolling even though things don't make sense. He can't help but noticing there hasn't been any sight of rival pride members near the border. The rival pride's intrusion would top off his madness. But not one has been seen for a long time. The vast-open-plain feels ominously quiet and empty.

In the den the adult lioness looks at her two still hungry adolescent daughters, feeling sorry that she could neither provide more food for them nor teach them how to hunt bigger game.

"When was the last time you saw a wildebeest or zebra herd grazing around here?" babbles the lioness. *"When was the last time we had a real meal?"*

To her anguish she has been seeing humans hunting more frequently the same prey. Their food source has become humans' subsistence. Alas! A lion is no match for humans who come with their vehicles and arms. Wildlife helplessly surrendered to the onset of their brutal slaughter.

While searching for prey she remembers that she had seen big, tempting herbivores grazing peacefully next to a human settlement.

"That's what I call a real meal. Perhaps, if I sneak in at night when villagers are sleeping, I may get lucky," mumbles the lioness. Taking her two young daughters she heads for the village.

These villagers are the Lozi people who live on the border of the Liuwa Plain National Park, where they grazed their cattle. As the Park is not fenced in predators can easily walk in. Our stealthy lioness enters the cattle enclosure, and to her delight the cattle do not take flight like other prey. She pulls her body towards the ground picking a calf as a target, and jumps on it. Howling, the calf alarms the farmer. *Boom, boom.* The farmer rushes out with his rifle and shoots the lioness. Immediately, her two frightened daughters only several yards away dart into bushes.

More shots arc fired from behind. The cubs are running, full-speed, for their life. Their feet barely touch the ground. Their bodies zip through, down the slope, up to the plains. Once they have run out of the danger zone, they stop and turn round to see if mom will emerge from behind. No sign of mom, not even a shadow in the moon light. They wait and wait till the dawn breaks.

"Sister, mom is gone. Death has snatched her," mumbles the big sister.

"I always thought mom was invincible. She would survive when no one else could make it," cries the young sister. *"Now what shall we do?"*

This tragedy of loosing their mom is an immense blow for the youngsters, for they are only about eighteen months old, neither quiet fully grown in body nor fully trained in hunting. Normally in a pride the mother raises and trains her cubs till they are fully grown which is about two years old. Then the male cub will be kicked out by the alpha male to find his own new territory, and the female cub can either stay—if the adults accept her—or she can leave like her brother to find a new home, forming a new pride. Most of the time, the females choose to stay with the original pride members. It is not uncommon that the kicked out male lion finds no new home and becomes a nomadic lion.

Sorrow filled their hearts, for the daughters love their mom very much. Back in the den they sniff mom's scent. A flood of memories flushes in their mind, especially those moments of intimacy between mom and cubs: suckling and nibbling mom's teats, tumbling over mom's back, chasing mom's tail as well as the no less important aspect of security that mom provided when menaced by intruders. Still in their mouth was the taste of mom's fresh kills. And after the meals who could forget the grooming time? They would spend 20 hours a day in their lie-up, licking, nuzzling, and rubbing each other, indulging themselves in a wonderful feeling of family bonding.

They remember how their mom taught them to hunt after they turned one year old. *"First, select your target; let your target be a proper size—nothing too big for your size. Then stalk your target; make yourself unseen by crouching and creeping, belly on the ground. Always stalk as close as possible. Then rally all your muscles and chase, all the while focusing on the target. Wrestle the prey to the ground with the strength of your fore-body and go for the throat to suffocate the animal with your jaws."*

They got to practice their hunting skills during a group chase, but were not experienced enough to be successful. Now they can only recall the memory of what they observed during a group hunt and rely on their instinct.

Mom was a stellar hunter, speedy and agile. She played the lead role in a group hunt. She was as much a good teacher as a good

16

discipliner. She wanted her cubs to learn how to hunt properly and not to waste energy. Not to mention—God forbid—injury or being killed. During a hands-on hunting lesson while mom and the aunts held onto a captured small prey, mom would nudge the shy cubs to come first and slap the aggressive one telling them to wait.

Now mom is gone; they are forced to think about where the next meal will come from. It is out of question to think about going out to hunt; besides, their spirit is broken. Their only hope now is their dad, for sometimes he does call out from the plains: *"Wuh-ooow, come here to eat!"*

Their dad, the alpha male, is out patrolling. He usually leaves hunting to mom and the aunts. His responsibility is to protect the lionesses and cubs from other predators. Not to mention guarding against the invasion of another pride. His work, occasionally, includes joining the hunt on buffalo. He will use his heavy weight and enormous power to subdue the bulky prey. The participation of a big male in subduing the prey usually tips the scale in favor of the lions. Yet male lions rarely join group hunting because male lions do not have the speed and agility as lionesses have. But, when threatened, he will lay down his life to defend his territory and family. Cubs are important to him because they are his future. When an old lion gets too weak to hunt or protect himself, the young will take care of him by keeping him in the pride to feed.

The alpha male is the head of the family; he leads and keeps the family members in order by laying down his rules and maintains his authority. The females and cubs show submission to him; he gets to eat the kill first, followed by the lionesses and the remnant belongs to the cubs. He may have a brother or brothers in the pride sharing the responsibilities. When the alpha male is too old to lead, the brother will dethrone him and take over the pride.

Back to the current status, our alpha male is stepping into a meet with his fate. The trophy hunters are in hot pursuit of him. They scored a victory in last hunting with one magnificent-male-lion trophy. But that wasn't good enough. They muttered, *"Too bad, the other one escaped. We will be back to hunt the escapee."* People with big bucks would pay a high price for male lion's magnificent mane. What an ostensive decoration for their home. Pompously, they like to show off their glorious victory. However, their interests undermine a pride's family structure and throw it out of balance. Lions are the only species that has a social structure which resembles a human family. Other herd animals form groups or clans, but only lions form families.

The alpha male is key to a stable pride. Without its protection, cubs are most vulnerable to other predators such as leopards, hyenas, baboons and other fierce animals like buffalo. These animals all want to kill lion cubs, for one less lion cub means one less lion and one less threat. Also, internally, without the authority and disciplines of the mature-adult-male lion, the juveniles' behaviors could become erratic and, sometimes, dangerous to their own pride. The lionesses benefit from his protection, too: he is the king of the beasts with his massive body, heavy weight, and powerful jaws. Just his posturing is enough to scare away other predators.

Will the alpha male ever be challenged? Yes, by his own brother or his own grown up son or by nomadic males. The most ruthless takeover is by a nomadic male lion. After the old alpha lion is defeated and chased away, the first thing the nomadic lion would do would be to kill all the cubs, for he would not want cubs sired by another lion. Without their cubs the lionesses would go into estrous again, and the new alpha male can father his own cubs. However, a generation of lions would be wiped out.

Boom, boom. The trophy hunter finds the alpha male and fires. Thud, drops a heavy body—THE LAST MALE LION IN LIUWA PLAINS BITES THE DUST.

Hunting

Three days past and the girls haven't seen their dad. He did not come home from patrolling. Their hunger reached an unbearable point. *"We will have to go out to hunt."* Both sisters get up, pad towards the open-plains, and scout for prey. Good. About one hundred yards away, a group of impala is grazing. They look at each other and know exactly what each shall do. Who can deny that animals possess some sort of telepathic ability that enables them to communicate? Without a language they can transmit their wishes in an imperceptible way. The strategy is, the fast one will chase; the other waits in ambush to catch the prey when it escapes. In their experience of hunting with their mom and aunts, their mom would always stalk the target and chase it towards their aunts who were waiting in ambush on the other side. So they would do likewise and the hunt begins.

Slinking along with their ears flatten, the big sister selects her target and stalks. Her tawny coat makes a good camouflage; she simply disappears in the tall golden grass. The target is unaware of her stalking. Yet there is always a sentry, be it a bird, a zebra, or a baboon, watches from the treetops, scanning the fields for any sign of a predator ready to blow its cover. As soon as she is discovered, the alarm sounds. Our lionesses leap to chase. The impala, highly reactive to any disturbance, picks up its spindly legs and flies in mid-air. Its strategy is to change direction frequently to get rid of the chaser. Poor little thing, this time its direction change leads it right into the paws awaiting in ambush. Frantically it turns round only to be jumped on by the big sister. The impala is taken down, and its throat is clamped down by the jaws, just what mom and the aunts would do to suffocate the prey. The little sister sinks her claws into its rump and starts gnawing.

The sisters are exhilarated with their first prize earned without the help of any adults. It was the will and necessity that drove them to do it right the first time. Intense concentration, rising adrenaline, a powerful sprint, and cooperation—all contributed to score a big victory. Now comes the easy part: how to eat the carcass. First, they open the impala between the hind legs, eat the guts and carefully bury the stomach, covering up all traces of blood (to avoid attracting vultures and hyenas). Then the big sister clutches the impala by the neck, straddles it between her forepaws, and drags it into a well-chosen spot, a shady brush. There they gorge the meat to their hearts' content.

"Sister, did you bury the stomach? Did you covered up all the blood traces? If not, you know what will happen?" the big sister questions.

*"You bet I know wha*t will happen. *Those prowling hyenas will pop in, jumping around with their horrible, shrilling giggles to claim the prize as if it were theirs."* The little sister's mockery is said with anger. *"What about the scraps for later? Do we do anything with them?"*

After a kill comes the problem of guarding the kill. Sometimes the latter proves to be a lot more strenuous. Now the vultures, circling in the sky, are descending and swarming in for their shares of the carcass. They are absolutely annoying, yet not as dangerous as the hyena pack. The big sister turns round and chases the vultures away, only to see them come back again. The vultures are relentless and plentiful; to chase them away is futile. They go back to gorge themselves, for they might not make another kill for another two weeks, or they might even loose this one to the hyenas—their mortal enemies.

Hyenas are fierce predators: their powerful jaws can crunch your bones and finish you up in minutes. As individuals, hyenas are cowards and no match for lions. Their strength comes from sheer numbers. Like lions, hyenas hunt in pack. Unlike lion pride having only a dozen members on average, hyena clan can have up to thirty or more clan members. And when their numbers are great, they can pose a serious threat to lions. Fighting hyenas are always on the agenda of an alpha male. His massive body, ferocious roar and fiery temper make quite an impression on hyenas. Our lionesses remember one time when they were harassed by a pack of hyenas who fought to steal the carcass, their dad, upon hearing the growls and grunts, rushed in. Taking one look at the hyena clan, he pounced on the clan's leader—an alpha female—and snapped her throat. With the bloody-lifeless corpse hanging in his mouth, the alpha male made a statement to the rest of the hyena clan.

"Great, no hyenas around, this time!" cheer the lionesses.

Now their stomach looks like balloons. There is still a lot of meat left on the carcass after their binge.

"What do we do with the remains, do we let the vultures have them?" asks the little sister.

"Absolutely not! We can drag it to our den where the bush is thick and the shade is dense." replies the big sister. She counts on the remains to feed them for three more days.

The Empty Den

Back in the den, they flop on their sides. As in the good-old-days they start their grooming ritual by rubbing against each other's head, licking off the blood, and assuring their affection and support for one another.

"Come, sister, let me lick off the blood behind your ears and on your back as well." Lab, lab. The big sister cleanses all the places that her little sister can't reach till not one dingy spot is left. She is the more affectionate one. She is also endowed with superior genes in terms of health, intelligence, and good nature.

The excitement of the chase and their first kill has tired them. Opening wide their mouths they yawn. *"Let's call it a day and go to sleep...."*

At dawn a splendid-silver sunrise looms on the African-plain horizon. Listen carefully to hear the birds chirping in the trees, the small ground animals rustlings in the weeds and gentle breeze. These are the only sounds that break through the air. Before the Angolan War, this land was filled with wildebeest, zebra, and buffalo herds; lions, leopards and cheetahs abounded. One would hear a symphony of "Click, clik, clik", "Moo—moo—", and "Eu, eu, eu"—song of the herbivores accompanied by the growling and grunting of the predators. All this vibrated across the plains. Now, only eerie silence.

Before these two lionesses were born, there were numerous lion prides in the Liuwa plains; some of the prides had up to 20 or more members. Those were the prosperous good-old-days that the young lionesses never enjoyed. This last pride of two adult males, four adult females, three litters, a total of eleven including the two young lionesses was the only pride they know. They, too, were disappearing, one by one.

Life has to move on. The cubs' playfulness was far from dead. They resume their cub-hood's rough-and-tumble: chasing each other up to the rocks, knocking each other down, and tumbling down the hill together. Still full of energy they dash over to a riverbank and scare away the pelicans and storks. Since they are not hungry they decide not to chase the birds.

Something catches their eyes; they are fascinated by the frogs croaking and sauntering about. Young as they are, full of curiosity and adventures, they would attack first and ask questions later. The lioness paw swoops down. To her surprise the frog is swift enough to leap away and escape. The chase is on. Both species dance about till the frog plunges into the water.

Water has become a matter of fact for the lions in the Liuwa plains because the region is under water for six months during the rainy season. Water is not a natural habitat for lions as it is for tigers in the jungles. Tigers swim and catch prey in the water. However, these lions living on the riverbank have adapted to water. They can wade, swim and kill in the water, and these cubs are as comfortable as fishes. They know how to have fun with water. Look at them bobbing with their paws, twitching their tails, and splashing water up to five feet high. Ducking and emerging, in and out of the water keeps them busy.

Slithering into the water a sixteen foot crocodile creeps towards the cubs. Crocodiles can be vicious. They are able to attack with lightening speed and kill animals bigger than their size. They are crafty and can plot their hunting behavior to match their specific prey. Not wanting to alarm the cubs this large crocodile submerges without a ripple and swims underwater towards the cubs. With a splash, emerges a huge-wide-open jaw laced with razor-sharp teeth ready to slam shut on one of the cubs. The agile cub leaps to the left and escapes the fearsome jaw. By a thin hair the cubs avoid becoming the big crocodile's dinner.

"Let's get out of here. That ugly thing scared the day light out of me. Mom was right, these monsters are cub-eaters," gasps the little sister while running.

Back on the riverbank the game continues. The cubs play hide-and-seek or ambush all the way to a nearby tree.

The big sister sinks her claws in the trunk and swiftly leaps to the upper branches. The slender branches bend dangerously under her weight. When she hears the branches crackling, she jumps over to the crown of the tree. Even there the boughs start to crackle. She turns quickly. Cautiously testing each branch, she heads down.

Plunk, she lands face down with her four feet sprawling outwards, not a dignified landing. Embarrassed she struggles up to her feet and jumps around her sister.

"Sister, now it's your turn to climb the tree," nudges the big sister.

The shy sister takes a deep breath, sinks her claws in the tree trunk, lifts her weight upwards, and reaches the top in a few leaps. Her lighter weight causes less crackling in the branches. Proudly she turns round and begins her descent. She lands gracefully with her forepaws on the ground first.

With a companion life is a lot more fun, and time flies by.

The lionesses are out. Once again driven by hunger they search for prey. A mature warthog wallows in the swamp mud. They look at each other and go for it. Warthogs, though, small in size (40 – 50 pounds for adults) have large upper tusks, which can be dangerous. Despite their short legs they surly can run fast and often do outrun the predator.

The big sister moves towards the warthog's head while the other sneaks from behind. With a frightening snort the warthog springs up and launches a preemptive strike—jabbing the lioness with his tusks. Her sister from the rear claws him on the rump. Immediately the warthog spins around to ward off the surprise attack. Now the big sister can lunge for the back, but the warthog whips around to strike. The spinning continues on and on until both parties are worn out. As soon as the warthog drops flat, both the lionesses jump on top of him claiming their prize.

****

Just when it seems these two sisters have the upper hand in the struggle for survival, nature shows its savage face once again.

Lazily, the big sister lies up in the shade while the younger sister ventures off into some nearby shrubs. She finds herself face to face with a spitting cobra. The cobra startles her but does not disinterest her. Her curiosity pushes her to investigate this funny looking creature. Fast as a flash, the cobra spits its venom right into her eyes.

"*Yelp,*" she cries in pain and runs off.

She can't see now. The spitting cobra's venom is deadly. Young cubs could die immediately. Adult lions have more body mass to cope with the poison, and even with that they have to wait for several weeks to let the poison pass through their system to get well. If the eyes are hit, blindness ensues till the body recovers. In other words, she has to get well first in order to see again. This venom in the eyes in this case is a death sentence to our lioness

The little sister staggers about in the wildness, not knowing where she is. The venom is taking a toll on her. Her light weight body cannot cope as well as the heavy build of an adult. Her legs are becoming feeble, and *plunk* she collapses on the grass.

Dusk sets in, opening the door for the sneaky, nocturnal beasts the hyenas. On by one, they close in from all directions. They sense something is wrong with this lioness. She offers no resistance….

"*Hurrah, easy meat tonight!*" The excited hyenas, holding their tails up and forward over their back, dance about and cheer with hysterical chuckles.

Gobbling, gobbling. Crunching, crunching. The hyenas devour their meal. All parts of the lioness are consumed in a few minutes, and the last trace of blood is licked up. The darkness of night engulfs the plains.

"Wuh-ooow, wuh-ooow—", calls the big sister. No response. *"Wuh-ooow, wuh-ooow—"*, the big sister calls again with a shaking voice. In between calls she opens her mouth and curves her upper lip to smell her sister's scent. No scent. And this has been going on for hours and eventually for days. Sadly, she is met only with silence—

"Please God, let my sister come home!" begs the sister.

This is what she would pray if she could pray, *"Please don't take my only companion away from me; I don't want to live alone; please let me live and live a life worth living!"*

Roaming and roaming, seeking out her sister, the lioness' roar echoes throughout the vast-open-plains. Here we have a sad, lonely lioness. WE CALL HER LONELY LADY LIUWA.

Courage

A cold stillness greets the only surviving lioness in the empty den. She doesn't know how many days she hasn't eaten. Her heart is broken; depression sinks in. She doesn't feel like getting up to find something to eat even though she is hungry. She lets herself be drowned in miseries, sadness and loneliness. Who cares? She has no one to care for, and no one is here to care for her....

What do you know? In a flash, a small animal dashes across in front of her eyes. It's a hare. Instinctively, she leaps and gives a chase. With one swat, the hare is done for. A meal self-delivered to her mouth.

This bit of food in her stomach gives her some energy opening up her appetite; she picks herself up and strolls out in search of more food. There, in the clearing a piglet has drifted away from its mom, easy meat for the lioness. Unknowingly, the piglet trots right up to the lioness. *Swoop*, the lioness pounces on the piglet. The piglet's squealing and squalling reaches the ears of the big warthog. She bolts in to rescue her child, only to see her baby's bloody body dangling in the lioness' mouth. She gives only a half-hearted chase because she knows it's too late to do anything now.

Once in a while Lady sees big game grazing in the plains: wildebeest, zebra, or eland. She doesn't have enough courage, yet, to tackle them. She isn't strong enough; she has no hunting partner. She turns to smaller game such as small antelopes, piglets, and storks.

Patiently, she waits to grow into a mature adult. She perseveres in stalking and in chasing prey even though only one out of five is successful. This is good exercise for building muscles, agility training, and developing judgment as to what prey to choose, in what distance to start the chase, and most of all when to quit, for an exhausted lioness is useless when next opportunity presents itself.

Lions are apex predators. One clamp down of their canine can sever an animal's spinal cord. Forepaws powered by a strong upper-body muscle can knock you down with one swat. Their claws are sharp as a knife. With one swipe, your flesh is shredded. However, because their claws have a retractable feature, they can play without incurring injury.

As Lady Liuwa gradually moves from small prey to larger prey like wildebeest and zebra, she would target the old and the sick. In doing so she helps shorten the suffering of the weak. Her favorite meat is wildebeest.

The most troublesome adversary she has is the hyena pack. They are forever present when a kill is made; they want to steal Lady's hard-earned prize.

Feeding on a fresh kill, Lady becomes aware of a swarming hyena pack. Lady Liuwa's exasperation kicks up her adrenalin when the hyenas circle in to bump her off the kill.

"You ruthless beasts, don't you know the Pecking Order? I guess I ought to teach you some manners," shouts Lady at her eternal enemies.

She snarls, bearing her canine to the roots. Rearing up, she stretches in an attempt to look big and tall. Rallying all her strength, she's ready for a big fight. At this moment, her energy level spikes. And this electrifying energy makes the hyenas shudder. One by one, Lady Liuwa lunges and swats the hyenas. To her advantage, a lone hyena has no guts to fight an adult lion. True to their cowardly characters, each tucks its tail between the legs, flat against the belly, and skulks away. Thus a lone lioness trumps a group of hyenas!

"Good! You all have learned your lessons today. Remember we lions are no pushovers. We fight tooth-claw for our prize." She stands her ground.

Battling for food has taught her that survival is for the fittest. One must hone in survival skills. Most of all, one faces the adversity with endurance, takes on the challenge with courage. Patience and concentration do pay off in the end. She has found the survivor's motto.

But her problem is not just food; something is missing in her life. *"Where are the boys?"* She remembers she saw one. It was like a mirage, *a male lion* walked into her gaze. His face was etched into her mind making it a permanent memory impossible to forget. This one strong, handsome male lion with an impressive dark mane was a passerby. A magnet drew her to this stranger. Her heart pumped fast and loud. She wanted to get closer to him, but her feet froze. She couldn't free herself from her own shyness.

Since the stranger was a stray lion, his mind was on *how do I get out of here*. He paid no attention to our lioness. His silhouette faded into the outstretched plains. She saw him no more, she only saw him once.

Day and night she roams and roams. *"Wuh-ooow, wuh-ooow, anybody out there? I want to share my life with you."*

Her calling is met with silence; not another lion has been seen in the vast Liuwa's plains. Nevertheless, she keeps on calling, for there is always tomorrow when a new day's horizon extends out to bring in a new hope.

First Encounter

A vehicle is roaring in the distance. Lying in the shade is Lady Liuwa. She looks up and sees a few hundred feet away this machine with special equipment progressing towards her. The vehicle stops. A man gets up and maneuvers his equipment, aiming it in her direction. Swiftly she shifts to a defensive mode, ears flatten and tail down, Lady bounces to her feet and sizes up the vehicle. The vehicle makes no move. She ducks and creeps towards the vehicle. When she would hunt, her first reflex would be to stalk the prey, but this is not a prey.

Vehicles are viewed by lions as part of the landscape. People inside the vehicles are considered as part of the vehicles. When people step outside, they are stepping into the lions' zone. Some lions will get defensive and attack.

Driven by an insatiable curiosity, Lady scans the vehicle and the crew. She sets out to watch the team's every move. She sees a cameraman who is standing in the front surveying the landscape with his zooming device. Other members are sitting behind, talking, and pointing. An over-sized, four- wheeled vehicle is something she has never seen before.

"Is this a creature, or is this part of the landscape?" Our lioness is trying to figure out what it is and how to interact with it. *"Wait a minute! Is this what I have been looking for?"* A light bulb just lit up.

She is searching for something that is missing in her life—love and companionship. How can she find love and companionship when every time she approaches another animal, even without the least intension of killing, they all run away? Although it is unnatural for a lioness to seek companionship with humans, under these circumstances these men are her only choice.

Now, her strong 6th sense is telling her that there is something fun and adventurous in encountering this vehicle.

"Wait a minute! I just remember how mom was shot by a two-legged being and how my sister and I nearly escaped the bullets. I also saw my uncle being fired by a man armed with rifle. I would be a fool if I should get close to these people. Let me watch them from a distance for a while." In her ambivalence she needs to convince herself that these people would do her no harm. She needs to at once observe their every move and keep a safe distance in case of any abrupt aggression.

In constantly going over the *pros and cons*, her opinion swings in favor of these two-legged beings. *"These people don't look like those lion hunters. They are calm, relaxed, and unarmed. Why are they here, I wonder?"* After a few more canny analyses our lioness' qualms are eased; her curiosity is kindled.

Inside the vehicle, the cameraman is ecstatic that a lioness walks right up to his lens. He wasn't expecting to see a lioness, a hyena perhaps but not a lioness. He cannot turn his head; his gaze is fixed on his lioness. The rest of crew is no less fascinated by this phenomenal sight on account of the presumption that the lion population in the Liuwa Plain was eradicated. All marvel with wide eyes and gasp, *"Look over there—a lioness out of nowhere!"*

Lady is taken in by the cameraman's gaze. This magic eye contact speaks so powerfully. *"This man is interested in me; I never had anyone paying attention to me like this. He looks like someone that I can trust."* She also feels privileged to be the center of the crew's attention. By now her ego is flattered and her sensitivity is soothed. She feels secure with the vehicle. Her mellowness surfaces as her defensiveness subsides. For the moment she is one relaxed, big cat ready for venturing into a new relationship.

Fully Grown

The lioness is now fully grown in her prime. She is beautiful. She has a rather round face as oppose to long face. Her large eyes are slightly slanted and honey color. The pupils are round and black. Her vision is empowered by a special coating that will reflect moonlight as much as starlight. When she stares at you, you feel you are being penetrated. She can spot prey hundreds of yards away.

With blobs of muscle she looks like a body builder. That's because she has only herself to depend on while hunting; she must do it right the first time or else. Her all-muscle-no-fat body enables her to be a powerful sprinter. She relies on her enormous muscle strength to take down the prey as well. A lion's top speed is 35 miles per hour over a distance of 100 yards. Although lions are powerful short-distance sprinters, they are not long-distance-marathon runners due to their hulking body. They have only one minute to catch their prey.

Her ears, standing in a triangle shape, swivel to hear sounds from different directions. She can hear a long distance away, far better than humans can. Her tail has a black tassel at the tip. The tail is, primarily, used to balance the body. It can also be used as a signal to other animals. When Lady isn't hunting, she would curl up her tail and strut around without a worry in the world; the other animals would know that they could lay down their alarm.

Her tawny coat is as soft as silk. When she crouches in the tall golden-grass field she disappears—results of millions of years of evolution and adaptation. As all warriors she has scars to show her hard fought battles. Her skin-deep scars demonstrate what a formidable fighter she is.

Like most carnivores, Lady is a digitigrade's walker—walking on their toes. But the majority of the body weight is borne by the main paw pads. Her claws are equipped with a retractable feature which helps keep the claws sharp and prevents injury during playtime.

Her sense of smell is well developed. She can smell a carcass one mile away. One interesting feature associated with her sense of smell is a special olfactory organ on the roof of her mouth called the Jacobson's organ. When she wants to smell she curves her lips to draw air over her Jacobson's organ. That's why she has a grimace on her face when she smells.

When she bares her canines, one would shiver. Her canines—two up, two down—are five times longer than the rest of her teeth. They are used to tear off flesh and can server a spinal cord. When Lady closes her mouth, her canines interlock and restrict her to an up-and-down chewing movement. While she eats she uses only one side of her mouth each time due to the inability of her jaw to move side-to-side. As a result she swallows her food rather than chewing it.

Her tongue is covered with rough quills, called papillae. This helps her scrape meat off the bones, and is used as a comb for grooming.

Unlike herbivores Lady's digestive system is simple, with short digestive tracts. Lady has an enormous stomach; she can swallow up to one hundred pounds of meat in one sitting. This allows her to fast for a week. Otherwise she would need to eat 15 pounds a day and to hunt every day.

****

Eu, eu, eu—, migration season is here again. The Liuwa Plain, now covered with new grass, looks like a green carpet stretching out endlessly. A herd of wildebeest indulges themselves with the finest food. Due to the highly nutrient food the birth rate is up. Newborns are numerous at this time of year.

Lady Liuwa is fascinated by the newborn. *"What a cute little thing."* Those enormous eyes and spindly legs captivate her. This attraction stems from the knocking of motherhood inside her. One young calf is separated from its mom. Lady Liuwa approaches, gazing lovingly; the inexperienced newborn stays still. At this very instant the line between a predator and motherhood vanishes, and eventually motherhood prevails. Retracting her claws, Lady bowls over the calf to cuddle.

"Yelp!" Lady screams in pain and leaps two feet.

Frightened by the unusual scene, the wildebeest mom rushes back to rescue her foal. The adrenaline pumps up in her blood, the brave animal charges Lady. Luckily the injury is only skin deep. Lady runs away, but the angry mom won't quit. To defend herself Lady turns around, snarling at the wildebeest. The fight is on.

The angry mom lowers its head aiming at the lioness ready to thrust its sharp curved horns. Lady leaps and dodges the would-be-fatal blow. In turn she jumps onto the back of the wildebeest, sinks in her sharp paws, holds onto the animal, and bites the back of her neck. The lioness' canine teeth slip between her vertebrae and break her spinal cord. Death comes immediately to the wildebeest mom. The execution is quick. There is no struggle from the victim.

Our lioness is impressed with her own strength. She is no longer a young novice; she is a triumphant warrior. Single-handedly she killed a mature wildebeest for the first time. No lioness has come to age until she kills a wildebeest. At the moment of that kill, Lady Liuwa is transformed into a mature adult.

In the Liuwa Plain the only other carnivore is the hyena. They are her competition for food. She knows them well. She is constantly conscious of their whereabouts, their multiple dens. She recognizes their faces and their different personalities. She has to learn to deal with them on individual basis. Of course the meanest is the alpha-female. To establish her throne she has fought her way up in the hierarchical struggle. Hyenas do not live in a loving family setting as the lions do. On the contrary, they constantly hiss and spit among themselves within the clan. However, they hunt in packs and they are efficient hunters. Only in hunting do they cooperate.

Lady keeps the hyenas at bay with her feisty determination. They respect her. She would challenge them one by one, taking advantage of the fact that individually the hyena is a coward. But she is savvy enough to retreat when hyena numbers are great. When food is plenty she doesn't fight as much neither. She would abandon the carcass for the hyenas or would allow jackals to eat side by side with her, exhibiting her generosity and good nature. She is the biggest in terms of size and heart. With the absence of elephants, rhinos, hippos, and buffalo in Liuwa Plain, her enormous body brands her as the number one—the Uno.

Befriend

Up until the first encounter with the vehicle, Lady's experience with the humans, including the villagers, has not been a positive one. The villagers—the Lozi people are farmers: breeding fish or raising cattle and goats. Occasionally, the on-foot villagers would spot Lady from a distance. When she was sighted, they would either run away screaming, or would brandish a big stick threatening her. She knows better not to go near the villagers, let alone entering the villager's livestock enclosure. She keeps herself away from humans. However, this vehicle is mysterious. People inside it behave differently. She can't help feeling attracted by them.

"Will I see these friendly people again? I do hope so," murmurs Lady. This is the first time in her life that she has sentimental feelings towards strangers that are Homo species. She doesn't know how to handle it.

To drown out these weird feelings, Lady Liuwa sets out looking for a flawless tree. She wants to sharpen her claws. The sharpening also cleanses out dirt from her claws. Whenever she would spot a tree trunk with wholesome bark, she would stop and sharpen her claws. Today she specially takes her time to find a perfect tree for her sharpening. She rambles and rambles and stops in front of an umbrella-shaped acacia tree.

"You make one terrific umbrella. As for sharpening my claws, who wants to polish on this 'corky' bark that is to flake in papery pieces?" mutters Lady and moves on to a better tree. After some time of seeking, she makes a second stop in front of a baobab tree.

"Your bark is smooth and solid enough, but who wants to climb up on those huge roots?" Lady is picky today. She is thinking of her new friends, she wants to impress them with her clean and sharp claws. Finally, she comes upon a sausage tree with strings of sausage-looking fruits hanging down its limbs.

"You sausage tree, your blossoms are showy and beautiful, your fruits are enticingly inviting, and I can see your bark is solid and intact." Lady is content with the sausage tree. She hops on the bark, sinks her claws, and carves downward.

****

A human settlement waits in the African hot sun. T-Shirts and pants wave in the wind. The generator's dull hum fades into the background. This strange sort of settlement is not far behind Lady's tree. She catches sight of it. With her newly sharpened and clean claws, she trots up to the site. There are five tents on the site which are not fenced in. She enters stealthily. No one is on site. She strains her neck to peek into the tents. She sees interesting stuffs: cots, clothes, chairs, equipment, buckets, etc. After poking her nose everywhere she lifts up her head, raises her upper lip and breathes deeply. Excitement surges inside her. Nothing unpleasant; everything interesting. Cool! She likes this place. And confidently she walks out of the campsite, back to her tree. She flings herself on the roots and dozes off until the roaring of a vehicle awakes her.

Several people jump off the vehicle right into the bustles of daily living. Some are eating; others drinking. After a day's work in the hot sun, one deserves a shady spot and a nice meal with a cool beer. They are unaware of Lady's presence. Not yet.

"Have you heard the rumor that a tourist lodge will be constructed in the area?" asks one guy. A hot topic for all.

"That's what I heard, too. Let's hope it is true. I am tired of living in a tent. I want my shower and toilet," echoes everyone.

"Hey! We have a visitor!" says one man with a glint in his eyes, pointing to our lioness.

Everyone stops talking and looks to where he is pointing. Indeed they see an enormous lioness crouching by the tree. One guy walks towards her, the others stay behind.

Lady wiggles with qualms. *"Do I run or do I stay?"* she asks herself. In her heart she calculates, *"If I stay, these people may beat me up like the on-foot villagers. If I run away, these people may turn out to be just what I have been looking for and my dream for companionship will be dashed."*

During this indecisive moment she is swayed by the calmness and gentleness of the man who walks towards her. She feels she can trust that man, so she makes no move. Then the man stops and walks away, thinking—

The man comes back with a bowl of water and offers it to Lady. She laps it up. These two gestures harmonize in trust. Lady nuzzles up to him and starts licking his hand. He, in turn, pets her on the head. The affectionate strokes continue for some time. Here, a friendship is magically established between a man and a beast.

The boundary is broken. She is so happy that she stayed instead of running away. Her life has a new note, a new chance. Now she has a new hang-out. This night she decides to sleep at the campsite. She lies down. First she nuzzles up to the tent and rubs the canvas to show how much she loves her new home. Then rolling on her back, with her belly up and her four paws dangling in midair, she rolls and rolls to show how happy she is. She opens her mouth wide to yawn, closes her eyes, falls asleep and purrs. Her guttural song resonates throughout the campsite.

People inside the tents hear Lady. They let her rhythmic purring hypnotize them to sleep. They feel honored that the queen of Liuwa is spending a night with them.

Since then the campsite has become Lady's second den. Tent people are her friends. Whenever she would see them in the field, emotions would overcome her. Swiftly she would leave off whatever she is doing, even the victory of a fresh kill, to greet her friends sitting inside the vehicle.

"Wuh-ooow, wuh-ooow. Hello, good to see you!" She would drop down on the grass and roll, roll and roll onto her back … In lion's language this is a sign of confidence and contentment.

The crew feels tremendously privileged that they are graced with such a rare sight of lioness behavior. One can't help being deeply moved by this delicate, lovely scene.

It is worth noting that lions, contrary to preconceived beliefs, are neither merely a bunch of roaring aggressors nor simply walking meat without any brains or feelings. They can be gentle giants, intelligent and affectionate. When you bond with them you are part of their pride, and they shower you with love and tenderness. They have feelings and they think. Their reaction reflects the manner you treat them.

The famous lioness Elsa in *Born Free* by Joy Adamson, Meg and Ami in *Part of Pride* by Kevin Richardson—all exhibit great capacity for love and trust. Lions would take their relationship with you to the level of risking their own life for your protection. One good example is the account of the Tarzan film actor rescued by his pet lion. In a devastating studio fire, the lion pulled the unconscious actor out of the fire and saved his life (in real life, not in film).

****

While Lady makes her places among the tent people, the African Parks (AP) management team is working on a rehabilitation program designed to restore and develop a secure ecosystem. Reintroducing lions to the Liuwa Plain is on the agenda.

An AP official, Simon, now hears about Lady Liuwa's plight. *"How is it possible that any lion survived given decades of wildlife decimation in the Liuwa Plain?"* He is struck by this fairytale-like story. He has always been fascinated by big cats since childhood and has a degree in Zoology. Lady's story kindles a flame of passion in his heart.

He says to himself, "*I got to do something about this to pay back the wrong we humans did to her species in the Liuwa Plain. In my plan of reintroduction of lions, Lady Liuwa will commence a line of lineage for the lion population in the Liuwa Plain. Yes, that will be fair game!*" He instructed his colleagues to notify him of Lady Liuwa's whereabouts.

"*Simon, Lady Liuwa is now showing up at night on tent site,*" says Mark, another AP staff.

"*What does she do there? How does she behave?*" asks Simon.

"*She befriends tent's people. She behaves like a pet, very sweet and gentle.*"

"*A lioness befriends humans? A wild animal makes its way into human living quarter and makes friends? This is incredible if not impossible,*" laughs Simon. He feels compelled to meet Lady in person. He asks tent's people to call him the minute Lady shows up.

He is taking a shower when the phone rings. Hurriedly he rushes to the phone leaving the shower running, water dripping down his wet hair, and, of course, standing all naked.

"*Hi, Simon, she is here.*"

"*Thank you, Jack, I'll be right there.*"

Like a fast-forward-motion pictures, Simon wraps up his shower, slips into his underwear, and puts on his shirt and pants. There he goes. Jumping into his truck, he drives over to the campsite. He pulls up to the camp, a cloud of dust rises in wake of his AP van. As he parks near a tall tree, the dust settles down. His heart is pounding faster and faster with each one of his steps, he scurries in but there is no lioness. As he is about to look into one of the tents, he hears *lap, lap*. Twenty feet to his left he sees Lady's head plunged in a water bowl. He was told about Lady's good nature. Lady is docile and friendly. However, her enormous, frightening size makes him drag his feet. Hearing his shuffling, Lady stops drinking and looks at him.

Her penetrating gaze freezes him. Under the influence of her eyes his instinct of flight or to fight pulsates in his blood.

"Think it over, think it over" reasons his mind. *"She is not here to harm people; she is here to befriend people,"* Simon says to himself trying to loosen up a bit.

Lady walks up to him slowly and deliberately. She pauses, as if she were waiting for a good gesture from Simon.

Taking a deep breath, *"Hello, Lady, want some more water?"* says Simon in a soft voice.

Lady responds. She licks his hand. Encouraged by this friendly gesture, Simon pets Lady's head, and moves on to stroke her huge body. Her massive musculature and fabulous presence is set off by the hot African sun. He is impressed. Yet, in this mammoth sized strength there is not a hint of aggression, only tenderness. She seems to enjoy his touch, for she starts rubbing her head against his legs.

"Wuh-ooow, wuh-ooow." She thanks Simon for his attention, and wants to tell him her story.

While Lady is still woofing telling her story, Simon turns round to speak to one of the tent's people.

"Jack, Lady is moaning about something. Have you noticed her doing this before and how often does she moan like this?"

"Yes, we have noticed. Lady has been doing this woofing in a low voice often at night on the campsite. We aren't sure what causes it."

"It is a cry of loneliness," Simon sighs. He had studied animal behaviors in school. Pity wells up in his heart, for he knows it was humans who had sealed her fate. Now she is seeking companionship from them. This paradox disturbs his sensible heart. Something must be done to rectify this unnatural situation.

Lady is seeking companionship from Homo sapiens. However, what she needs is a mate of her own kind—a male lion. Nothing is more natural than to mate, to give birth, and to form a pride. The AP department has been considering the reintroduction of lions to the Liuwa plains. A particular mandate is to carry on the unique genetic line of Liuwa lions on account of cultural belief. To achieve this, translocating lions related to that of Liuwa's from elsewhere to breed with a local lioness is a perfect plan.

"She fits in like a key. I can't ask any better," proclaims Simon. Lady is like a gold nugget dropped out of the blue sky into his laps. In his elation, Simon moves up the schedule of the reintroduction plan.

The Park's Plan

When humans—Homo sapiens—lived on earth as cavemen during the Stone Age, their very survival depended on whatever nature provided. They were no better off than the other species. As Homo sapiens evolved, it evolved into a uniquely successful species who dominated all the others on earth.

When was human dominance forced over the other species? Did it begin with cultivation of certain edible plants and the farming of certain animals? The dateline is blurry. However, their ecological supremacy is a rather recent phenomenon. Only within the past hundred years by the technological advances did humans overcome the many obstacles that had previously plagued them. Now is the time of victory where they reap a colossal success in population growth and the expansion of the human habitat.

Human-vs-wildlife, an eternal conflict beginning with land where human's technical superiority pushes wildlife further and further into the remote wilderness. The conflict does not stop here. There are insatiable appetites for exotic animal products such as Chinese medicinal usage of animal body parts. Poor Tiger. Poor Rhinos. Don't forget about artifacts made from ivory and clothing made from hide or fur. Those, who are looking to satisfy culinary adventures, have created a new meat industry, also known as the hunting business. Hunting with bullets does not leave any chance for the wild animals. Some species were stalked down to near extinction. Others disappeared forever.

In the late eighteenth century and the early ninetieth century the U.K., the U.S.A. and the U.N passed laws in an attempt to rescue endangered wildlife and to restore the damaged ecosystem. These laws prohibited illegal poaching and established national parks as well as associated protected areas. All intentions were directed towards man's taking control in the balance of power in the wild. That is to say through the management of national parks, the conflict between humans and wildlife will be resolved in a positive way.

Today, humans are not like their ancient ancestors who had little control over their own destiny (and often fell victims to primordial predators). Modern people can have a great deal of impact, if not total control, in the shaping of environment and animals lives.

After a look at the bigger picture, let us return to the local scene. The African Parks Network, a non-profit company is responsible for the rehabilitation and long-term management of national parks and other protected areas which are public-private partnerships with the African Governments. This approach combines world-class conservation practices with business expertise, placing the emphasis on achieving a financial sustainability of the parks principally through tourism and associated private enterprises. These projects also serve as a foundation for economic development and poverty reduction.

The African Parks Network (APN) was founded in 2000 by a group of experienced conservationists (Mavuso Msimang, Dr Anthony Hall-Martin, Michael Eustace, Peter Fearnhead and late Paul Fentener van Vlissingen), who were concerned about the development of many of Africa's national parks. In just nine years, APN has taken on responsibility for the management of 5 protected areas in four different countries.

The Liuwa Plain National Park has been managed by the African Parks Zambia (APZ) since August 2003. The APZ holds a partnership with the above mentioned APN and the Zambia Wildlife Authority (ZAWA) and the Barotse Royal Establishment (BRE) (which is the traditional authority local communities.)

Liuwa Plain was accredited as a national park in 1972 and has one of the oldest wildlife protection histories in Africa. It was originally declared a royal hunting ground and a game reserve by the Litunga (the King) Lubosi Lewanika in the 19th century. The Lozi people were originally placed in the park by the Litunga as his official game keepers and their strong system of traditional rites, rules and regulations still exists today. 20,000 local people in four hundred thirty-two villages still have all rights in the park and it is not unusual to see people herding their cattle or fishing as their ancestors did. These activities can involve up to 100 people at a time.

In compliance with the African Parks Network (APN), Liuwa Plain Nation Park restoration-plan-layout centers on:

- To restock wildlife
- To control illegal poaching
- To gain community support for wildlife conservation and management
- To generate income and ensure the restoration program
- To ensure the development and implementation of efficient management systems

The good news is the results up to date have been far greater than expected on all counts. For example: Wildebeest numbers have gone from some 15,000 in 2003, to over 33,478 in 2007; Zebra 4,000 (2,800 in 2005); Red Lechew 1,167 (966 in 2005); and Tsessebe 501 (430 in 2005).

The account would not be complete if we did not mention the several successful translocation efforts of 49 elands, 60 elephants, 5 black rhinos, and 16 buffalo.

On the financial front—sustainable business for local communities is one of the goals of APN in Liuwa. For this end four communities have established their own campsites within the park. These facilities are one hundred percent community run. The profits generated stay in the business communities. These ventures are already self sufficient and will prosper with the increase number of visitors to the park. All this is done while the park continues to recover.

Safaris are making a comeback. The Zambian safari industry offers tours timed to see the best in November and December and again in May and June. Migrant water-birds fill the seasonal lagoons on the floodplain during these times. The blue wildebeest, now 34,000 strong in numbers, have returned from their northern migration to Angola, attracted by Liuwa's rain-fed new grass. October through

November is their foaling season. Liuwa safari focuses on the small but essential parts of a wildlife discovery such as examining the subtleties of an ecosystem, learning the names of trees, plants, fruits, seeds, insects, and birds, etc. Wildlife that can be observed include: wildebeest, zebra, lechwe, orbi, and spotted hyenas. What about the lions? A translocation plan is just underway.

First Attempt

The AP management team is meeting in the head quarter in Matamanene to discuss what to do to translocate a male lion to Liuwa Park. Despite the head quarter being a remote outpost, the modern equipment and Hi Tech gadgets are not lacking here. There are a huge display screen up front, hosts of computers sprawling around. Cell phones, lab tops, and GPS are personal carrying items.

Presiding over the meeting is Simon Clark, an APN manager in the Liuwa Plain. Present at the meeting are: Carl Thompson, a veterinarian; Jon Richardson, a park coordinator; Jack Milupi, a photographer; Mark Bartells, a ranger; Paul Mushibwe, a ranger.

Jon is in charge of surveying the existing wildlife in the Liuwa Plain and inputting the results into the data base. Nothing pleases him more than seeing the count goes up in the data base. And he is excited to announce, *"The data base tells me there are a good number of lions in Kafue."*

Kafue is about ten hours traveling in truck. But, why Kafue lions? Why not translocate lions from the Serengeti, for example? To understand the Park management's choice one needs to know Liuwa's local legend.

A little off to the west of Matamanene woodland in central Liuwa and at the heart of Lady Liuwa's home range, lies a small woodland island that is the traditional burial ground of the Induna Siyenge. The Siyenge clan is one of the original groups of people given the responsibility of safeguarding the wildlife of Liuwa by King Lewanika in the 1800's. Tradition has it that whenever an Induna from the Siyenge clan dies he must be buried in this woodland. On the first night after his burial it is believed that the lions of Liuwa come together, stand vigil and roar mourning for the deceased. After a few days a sacred grub emerges from the body of the deceased sprouting to the surface where it is transformed into a lion! It is for this very reason that the return of the lions to Liuwa is such a culturally important event. The loss of this keystone species would have effectively represented the loss of an important component of the local culture.

Hence, it is essential to select lions whose genetic line can be traced to Lady Liuwa. And they found one in Kafue National Park. The translocation is underway.

Translocating a wild animal isn't an easy task; it can be dangerous. It takes preparation and coordination. First, before a male can be brought in, Lady Liuwa has to be collared, so that the AP team can track her moves and find her in case anything goes wrong.

There are a number of concerns with regards to this process. How will Lady react to being darted, will it be a shock for her? Will her trust in man be shattered, terminating her new found friendship? We don't want to turn her into an aggressive lioness who hates people.

What about the sedative? It is risky. Sedating a wild animal can be a traumatic experience, if not deadly. With too much tranquilizer, you can kill the animal. We certainly don't want a dead lioness. Not enough tranquilizer, the lion in a stupor state can react erratically and kill you. We don't want to take that risk, neither.

The team is skittish, but, not for long. *"I will personally provide our lioness with special care to ensure a safe tranquilization process. We won't leave her until we are sure she is all right,"* affirms the veterinarian.

The meeting continues on, they tackle all the details from vehicle availability to securing a release enclosure. Simon is happy with the meeting's outcome. Now they have a concrete plan, next step is the implementation. First they need to find Lady Liuwa and administer anesthesia. According to the vet's calculation morning is the best time. The sun won't be so hot, and the team will have all afternoon to monitor Lady's condition.

With the motor drowning out the morning symphony of the Liuwa Plain, and after downing the first cup of coffee, the team, alert and anxious, jumps into the vehicle. The search for Lady is on.

Jack, the photographer, says to the vet, *"I admire your dedication and skill to the well-being of the animals. I wish I could do more for their cause. It bothers me when I see one sick or injured, yet unable to help."*

"True, you can help with neither sickness nor injury, but you are helping them in a different way. Your filming production is making its way, thousand miles away, to the living rooms of households worldwide. With the appreciation of wildlife, coupled with the awareness of their plight, humans will be committed to better caring of them."

"I certainly hope so...." A glint in the photographer's eyes.

Lady is found in her usual lie-up—a huge log from a fallen tree, a place provides at once with cover and shade. She walks out immediately when she sees the vehicle approach. She waits for her friends to get closer, so she can greet them. Guess what... As soon as the vehicle stops, instead of a greeting, *whuff*, a shot is fired at her. Her body shudders. She looks at her friends with a puzzled expression on her face. *"Why do you hurt me when you are my friends?"* Before she can figure it out, *flop*, she collapses on the ground.

"Perfect! She is down. Let's go." The team moves swiftly. While the veterinarian monitors the Lady's condition, the ranger fits the collar around her neck. A quick medical examination was done by the vet. He gives Lady a clean bill of health. *"Incredible! Our lioness is in excellent condition in spite of all the odds stacked up against her,"* remarks the vet.

Jack whispers into Lady's ear, *"We hate to do this to you, but we got to do it for your own good. Please understand and continue to trust us. Just trust us one more time, and we promise that your day will come."* The other echoes, *"We know what you want, and we will get it for you. Trust us, you beautiful thing."* And he kisses our lioness on the cheek.

Everybody has grown fond of Lady. All are concerned with the outcome. They hope by talking to her sweetly, while she is unconscious, her friendly attitude towards humans will remain upon awakening from anesthesia.

After the task is completed the team retreats to the vehicle to wait for Lady's recovery. The time seems to have stalled. The vet keeps switching his glances from Lady to his watch. Only the inhalations and exhalations of the nervous crew break the silence. Indeed, this is a moment of suspension!

"What is like to be tranquilized?"

"Want to try?"

"Look, Lady is moving!"

"Oooz, what's going on here? I got a huge headache." Gradually Lady regains her consciousness. Lethargically, she gets up. Having difficulty recovering her balance, she staggers a few steps. Finally, she walks with firm steps. Her rump stings. She tries to recall what happened to her, but her mind won't cooperate. She moves away from the vehicle and continues padding down to another zone. At night when her thoughts become clear, she probably will not remember the incident.

"Is she all right?" one staff asks the vet.

"Judging by her steady and progressive movement, she seems all right. I see nothing wrong with her. The recovery is perfect."

A big relief for the team, they are elated. The collar they put on Lady is transmitting the signal to the receiver. The team cheers. This signal marks a significant milestone for their project. Now they are looking forward to the next step of the plan.

A truck is ready for the journey to Kafue. Necessary equipment and items are checked off. Contact is made with Kafue National Park personnel. The second step of the process is rolling off.

A team of rangers, the veterinarian, a driver, and the photographer head out to Kafue in search of a perfect male lion to be the groom of Lady Liuwa. The atmosphere is light.

"I never thought I would become a match maker." says Simon.

"I know what you mean. I feel as if I were to give my own daughter away at the wedding bell," concurs Jack.

"Jon, I hope your data base is accurate. I hate to hustle about for nothing," says the driver.

"Let me say this: I would put my name on it," Jon stares down the driver, *"and to be precise, lions are reported to have been sighted in an area where quarries are."*

Quarries are lion's favorite hang-out, for they can hide behind the rocks as effectively as they can use them as a lookout. Therefore, it is a perfect place to find lions. As for our purpose, it is a perfect place for luring lions to come out.

After nightfall, an audio recording plays the roaring call of a lioness over the valley, offering an irresistible promise of mates.

"My lady deserves nothing but the best. I mean her mate should be a strong, handsome five-hundred-pounds," says the photographer.

"You'll get your chance of getting plenty footage of them and perhaps cubs, later on," says the vet jokingly.

The first night, there is no sight of a lion responding to the call. After all night of playing till dawn, the calling-for-mate plot produces no results. No males took the bait. The crew cannot believe that not even one lion showed up. The Liuwa Park staff wonders if the location chosen is the right one.

They ask their partner from Kafue Park who was responsible for providing the information. *"Are you sure of your reporting that this is the location of the lions hang-out?"*

"Positive. I can show you lion spoors leading to the quarries," says the Kafue ranger.

Getting out of the truck, both rangers inspect the dirt road. *"Yeah, I do see enough of fresh lion spoors leading to the quarries."*

The second night, still nothing. The crew is anxious now. Disputes erupt among them as to whether they should move to a different location.

"All right, the lions may have hung around in this area, but two days have passed, there is not even a silhouette of a lion, what does that tell you? Doesn't it tell you that they may have another hang-out? What does your data say about a second hang-out?"

"Patience, everyone, patience. My data does tell me there is a second favorite spot for the lions, but we may miss out on them by switching to the second favorite spot. Suppose the lions appeared at this location after we have left? Would you kick yourself?" Jon finds himself defending his position, hoping his rationale will help calm down the crew. After a second thought, the crew decides to stay put.

The third try is a charm. Lo and behold, there appears a male lion—a perfect match. Young-healthy looking lion with a short-blond mane. The veterinarian aims at the target and, *whuff*, darts the lion with a sedative. *"Good, right on target!"*

Excited, the team hauls this four hundred pounds body onto the truck, and starts the two hundred eighty miles and eleven hours journey to Liuwa. In Liuwa a release enclosure has already been prepared for their arrival.

It was an exhausting and grueling journey for the team. That doesn't lessen their being wary of the lion's physical condition. While the lion is still under anesthesia he is scrutinized carefully by the vet, and he seems to be in his best state.

The male is transferred from the truck onto a stretcher then placed inside the enclosure. A piece of meat is left for him to feed upon awakening. Then the pooped team goes to sleep.

Early in the morning, lingers African's residual night chill. Liuwa birds' chirping awakes the sleepy heads of the team members. A day like this would be perfect for a cup of coffee, but no one gives it a thought, they all hurry to check the lion. Can you image their expressions when they find him dead inside the enclosure! Tragedy strikes again, OH NO!

Both Simon and the vet examine the body for clue as to the cause of death. *"Hmmm, what could have killed a strong, healthy lion overnight?"*

"I see no exteriors injuries. However, let me check inside his mouth," the vet says, *"there you go, I see the culprit—a piece of meat clogged in his throat. He was suffocated to death."* The vet continues, *"This is what happened. At night, during the lion's recovery from anesthesia, and when he was still groggy he found the meat left by the staff and swallowed it. Since the journey and the enclosure were both so upsetting to him, in panic, he choked on the partially regurgitated meat."*

With heavy hearts, the staff cremates the lion's young-beautiful body. Anguish and guilt hang over them. They can't help feeling guilty in face of an innocent death, even though, they all have worked so hard for a noble cause.

Some says a prayer, *"God, let not our hard work go in vain."*

Other says, *"We need courage to go on."*

Everyone is depressed. *"Do we try again, or do we give it up?"*

Shortly after the cremation Lady Liuwa appears. She walks in sniffing. *"Where is he? I smelled him miles away, but where is he?"* wooofs Lady in a quivering voice. She pads up and down inside and outside the enclosure, only to find nothing.

She throws herself on the ground and mourns, *"Wuh-wooow, where is my boy, we could have lived a happy life together—"*

People are startled by Lady's unexpected appearance. Animals have an uncanny 6th sense, knowing what's happening from a distance away, or things that will happen in the near future. Lady is no exception. Her 6th sense and smell brought her here. She came with a hunch that something magical was about to break through and that her dream of being with someone—most likely a male lion, judging by the scent—was about to come true. Now, that something magical which was almost at hand had vanished. Her dream of having a mate and motherhood is shattered. She cries and cries—

Lady's disappointment and mourning deeply touches people's hearts. The AP team is now more than ever resolved to execute another translocation attempt. Except this time, it must succeed.

The Release Enclosure

The AP team studies the first attempt's failure, and comes up with a solution to the problem. The eleven-hour journey in the truck is too long for anybody, including animals. Waking up and finding yourself in a strange place is terrifying. Being unable to escape the confinement is just devastating. The first meal, the breakfast, needs to be supervised.

To alleviate the long journey, they will take a different route. This time they will drive the truck from Kafue to Mongu, and, then, will ride the boat from Mongu to Liuwa. This way, the truck ride will be cut down by five hours; the boat ride is only one hour and fifteen minutes. The management of the anesthesia will be different as well.

This time two lions are sought so that they can support each other's psychological well-being. When you have a buddy next to you, psychologically, you are strengthened. Besides, those hyenas, the cub killers, are rampant in Liuwa plains. Two lions would be necessary for protection. The AP team wants the pride to have the greatest chance to grow and to prosper.

To ensure the success, the AP team studies the weather patterns closely. May is the end of the rainy season. Water is still plentiful; flooded plains surrounding the Park will deter the new lions from escaping. You can't forget about their homing instinct. The high water will keep them safe and sound in Liuwa, at least long enough to settle down in their new territory. Prey is abundant at this time of the year, more delicious meat to add to their banquet table. All is staged to have a happy lion pride in Liuwa.

Before heading out for Kafue the team runs a check list:

- The release enclosure in the Park - secured
- An aircraft - booked
- All personnel - arranged
- Airstrips - cleared

- Veterinary requirements - met

All preparations are made well in advance. Pressure begins to mount as D Day approaches. The possibility of failure has to be excluded!

The second trip to Kafue is more serene. Simon's mind keeps running the scene of first attempt and its tragic outcome. Lonely Lady's heart-wrenching mourning resonates in his ears. In his mind he is determined to bring two lions back safely to Liuwa at any price.

This group's dedication in bringing back genetically linked lions and in restoring lion prides is indeed a work of redemption for humanity's previous brutality towards wildlife.

With better knowledge and high technology, humans, nowadays, could and should provide wildlife management. Herein I hasten to say, *"Lions are surprisingly human!"* Their pride resembles a human family; they nurture the young, feed the sick, and provide a place for the old. Astonishingly humanlike, lions want to love and to be loved. Intelligence wise, they are capable of learning, interacting and self-control during training or playing. It is only right to treat them with love and respect.

The team has gone back to the old quarries where the first lion was captured. Again after nightfall the team repeats lioness' calling. The roar is loud enough to be heard all over the valley. Will their attempt to lure any male lions out by an irresistible promise of mating work?

The first night, nothing. This time the team waits patiently.

The second night: *"Two males show up, look there is another one, wait, again one more. Making a total of four lions,"* the team shouts excitedly, they are pointing out the oncoming lions to each other.

Hastily the vet scans the four males and selects the two younger ones. He targets the chosen two males with his dart gun and fires. *Whuff. Whuff.* One lion drops immediately, the other drops while running.

Thrilled, the team of six heaves the lions from the rocks, and places them on the stretcher. Carrying the stretcher to the truck, they roll the sleepy lions into the pickup's bed. This seamless transfer can only be attributed to their team-work.

Being careful not to over drug the lions, the vet administers an antidote to the anesthetic at 10 pm. At 1 am the crew sets off for Mongu. At dawn the crew arrives in Mongu. During the trip the lions are darted with some more tranquilizers. Then the two lions are unloaded from the truck and reloaded onto a speedboat in Mongu harbor. The transfer was quick and efficient without a snag. The crew wants to keep the tumult as little as possible for the lions, for lions under anesthesia are susceptible to the slightest disturbance and can become sick or dangerous.

As expected Mongu harbor is filled with curious onlookers looking to catch sight of these two who have become famous by media broadcast. Most local villagers have never seen a lion. They want to see the king of the beasts, this majestic creature with their magnificent mane.

"Wow, how magnificent and gorgeous!" onlookers let out their cry and scramble for a closer view.

The crew pushes the crowd back and takes off quickly. The trip across the floodplain proves to be an easy sail. After an hour-fifteen minutes race the speedboat arrives at Kalabo.

Time is essential. The crew must speed up now, for the tranquilizer is wearing off, and the males will be revived soon. They must get to the boma (release enclosure) and release the males before they awake. If not, the consequence can be dangerous and deadly. Of course before their releasing, one of them must be collared, so that this coalition can be monitored, and action could be taken to apprehend them should the lions try to escape back to home.

There, in Kalabo the lions are loaded onto a Land Cruiser and driven to the boma near Matiamanene in the Park. This area is chosen because it is in the center of Lady Liuwa's home range.

On their way, the males are gradually coming out of the anesthesia. They are so groggy that they can barely move. The two lie side by side in the truck. The collar is fitted on one of the males. In a few minutes the Land Cruiser shall arrive at the destination. Everyone is tense because the drug induced stupor can act unpredictably, and any type of stress can shock them into some unwanted behavior. Minutes seem like eternity. Everybody in the vehicle is nervous. No one talks, there is only silence. Finally, they reach the destination.

There, quickly and quietly the team unloads the lions into the release enclosure. One at a time, the lion is rolled over from the Land Curser onto a stretcher, and then is carried by six people. The porters' adrenalin reaches the zenith. All exert their strength at the maximum level. After both lions have been rolled from the stretcher to the ground inside the boma, elation enwraps the team. Mission accomplished!

The entire capture and transportation phase of the operation was a resounding success with seamless transfers between the various modes of transportation. With much excitement, the team congratulates one another.

The plan is for the two lions to stay in the boma for about two weeks, allowing them to get used to the new environment. The team hopes this will calm their mood so that there will be no sign of ferociousness or aggression. Only after they have settled down will the staff release them to meet Lady. For now to ensure the safety for all, the release enclosure is fenced with electric wires.

The veterinarian thoroughly examines the males. Both are in excellent condition. No sign of trauma due to the journey. The lions are lying peacefully. By tomorrow morning they should be fully recovered. The exhausted team, then, goes to bed with high hopes.

An hour later, the males open their eyes and find themselves in a strange environment. Both struggle to their feet and try to stand up, only to fall back down due to their spinning heads. Slightly sore all over their body and the inability to muster their muscle causes them to yelping and moaning all night long.

At dawn, as soon as the coalition is fully recovered, the males nervously pad up and down the enclosure. They don't like what they see. They have never been in confinement in their whole life. Fear grips them. Instinctively they want to break the fence and escape. But when they charge the fence, they are zapped by a high voltage shock. What a surprise for the lions! Furthermore, their madness is only aggravated by the deterrence, and they continue to bang their head against the wires till they see that their efforts are useless.

Simon, being the most concerned gets up early in the morning, and rushes to the boma to assess the situation. He is relieved by the fact that the males are up and pacing. Despite their agitation and the grazes from attacking the fence, he sees that they are unharmed and healthy. As hoped, the two comfort each other.

The staff throws two big chunks of meat over the fence. They fill the water basin inside the boma. The males' aggression subsides. They are now eating breakfast. The happy crew, relieved that no complications have been provoked, gazes upon their victory.

A New Horizon

A lion's growl trembles the Liuwa Plain. A strange lion's scent fills the air. Lady Liuwa sets out to investigate. In spite of her last disheartening experience, she keeps her hope up. She follows the sound and scent leading her up to the boma (release enclosure). Lo and behold, two male lions inside the boma. She is entranced! Two young-handsome males each with a blond mane! Her exhilaration knows no bound. She sits down quietly as her tail waves in contentment. Her eyes are fixed on the males. *"Is this real? Pinch me, am I dreaming?"*

These two, startled by her appearance, instantly, take off with growling and grunting, lunging at Lady only to be stopped by the fence. Their reaction is typical for lions. Strangers are always perceived as a threat. For lions the best defense is offense.

"Who is she, is she here to attack us?" they ask one another. The males are totally taken in by the surprise visit of the lioness. They look at each other to seek support and say, *"We are a coalition and we would fight you in joint force should we be attacked."* They positioned themselves for a battle. In lions' fighting scheme posturing is half of the battle. The higher your temper flares up, the better is your chance to scare off your rival without engaging in a physical fight. No lion wants to waste energy nor takes the risk of being injured. All the two males want to do is to scare away Lady.

"Wuh-ooow, wuh-ooow, calm down, I'm not here to fight you; I'm here to help you," assures Lady with a soft voice, all the while seizing up the new comers for signs of further aggression.

"What, what are you saying? You are here to help us?" dumbfounded, the two males stammer.

"I have been waiting for lions to pass by to make friends since my sister's disappearance. My waiting has been five long years. I live alone in this vast land with countless hyenas.

I need the support of my own kind to ward off their marauding behaviors."

"Hyenas," the boys shout, *"we can't have enough fun kicking their ass. We give you our words that we'll protect you from the vicious hyenas."*

At the thought that Lady is not a foe but a potential ally, all their defensiveness dropped. The coalition is overwhelmed by the appearance of this beautiful lioness. They are trying to make a connection between the present situation and what transpired before.

Now they remember they were responding to a lioness's call for mating, and then it was a black-out. Is this lioness their promised bride—or is she not? *"Can you tell us what is happening to us? Why are we brought to this strange place? The last thing we remember was a lioness' call from behind the rock—our usual hang-out. Then a sting in our rumps followed by a black-out."* ask the boys urgently.

"I suppose humans brought you here. I'm not sure why they brought you here, but I believe they mean you no harm. I trusted them and I have made friends with them. I want you also to trust them and make friends with them," whispers Lady in a sweet voice, trying to convince these boys.

"But we hate to be confined. We want to be free, to wander off in the field like a lion. Can you set us free?" plead the two males with their begging eyes.

"I'll see what I can do. But, first, let me inspect the surrounding," replies Lady.

Then Lady prowls up and down outside the enclosure to see if there are any loose wires so she can turn it into a hole. All the wires are tightly interconnected. What about jumping over the fence? The fence is too high. Besides, she saw how the lions got zapped by an electric discharge whenever they touched the fence wires. It's not a good idea.

Lady babbles, *"We just have to dig a hole in the fence and escape that way. That means, first, we dig the dirt underneath the fence, and then we gnaw through some wires."* To do this she prefers to wait till nightfall when no staff is around. She wants to cause no hassle with humans. (Lions are crafty in playing innocent to get you off your guard.)

"How clever! We'll start tonight." The boys are pleased with Lady's scheme.

When night falls they start digging and gnawing. Initially they get zapped by an electric voltage, but once one wire is broken, the rest is easy. So, the job is in progress.

During the day time Lady lies down by the fence, accompanied by the two boys. The males are calm and settled. There is no more restlessness. AP staff reports the males' aggression has turned into interest; fear to complacency. A contented trio spends most of their time together. Everything seems to be running smoothly according to Park's Plan.

****

On the third day, the staff discovers the broken wires and makes an attempt to repair it. When the staff moves in with a vehicle as their cover, the lions react with a great deal of aggression.

"Oh, No! Our escape plan is discovered. We must stop the people from repairing the broken wires." cries out the coalition in anxiety. The lions stage an attack to foil the repairman with their ferocious growls while lunging at the vehicle.

"Stop it, the guy is only trying to do his job," yells Lady at the boys. Lady doesn't like any aggressive behavior for nothing. She has established trust with the Park's people. She sees no need on the part of the males to overreact.

How uncanny that the boys calm down right after Lady's yelling, but the repair guy do not dare to stay any longer. He leaves hastily with a half-job done. On the part of the team their logic is that it's better not to repair the broken electric wires than to put the animals through a great deal of stress. Stressing the animals would only defeat their purpose. So far the team has partially met their goal—the lions are interacting amiably. Creating any disturbance is just uncalled for.

By the fifth day, Lady has been showing up every day. She absents only to hunt. The lion group is very cozy with one another. The AP personnel are delighted that things are going so well. Another week, the lions will be released to form a pride, perhaps with couple new born cubs.

That night the trio is thrilled because the hole is getting big enough for them to escape. In a few moments the prisoners shall regain their freedom. The minute the boys have finished chewing up the wires, they squeeze themselves through the hole. Lady hurries to escort them out of the enclosure area. *"Come, follow me to the right!"*

Three shadows flicker through the woods in the moon light. Birds seated on tree branch bridges are peering down with incredulity at the lion group as they run below, snapping dry wood with their heavy paws. Squirrels dash away to clear the path at the sight of the trio. All the small animals are amazed by what they see—a group of lions, something unseen before.

"I think we are far away enough from the enclosure. Let's stop and catch our breath," says Lady panting. Looking over her shoulder she verifies that the enclosure is out of sight.

"Terrific, what about resting by those huge trees? They make good covers for us."

Next morning—the sixth day, when the crew visits the enclosure they are shocked to see it empty. Lions are no where to be seen. They run up and down, only to find a big hole in the fence. Obviously, the lions have gnawed off more wires and escaped. Adding to their agony, there is no sign of Lady.

Seized by fear and anxiety the crew, immediately, sets out to look for the lions. Hopefully they are not too far away. Suppose they escaped towards Angola, which is out of collar range, then it would mark, yet, another disastrous translocation failure. God forbid.

The probable devastating outcome drives the crew to act as fast as they can before it's too late. They follow the collar's signal and in few hundred yards they find the lions—the trio.

Lady Liuwa is on her back rolling with her four paws dangling in the air, turning her head towards the boys who lie opposite of her a few feet away. She lovingly keeps an eye on them. The boys seem to enjoy Lady's flirtation. They, too, cast a loving gaze upon her. That moment is an eternal magical moment!

"How beautiful, how gracious she is," blurt out the boys in admiration. At that moment these two grateful males have given their whole heart to Lady. She is their queen. They are her chevaliers from now on.

When Lady gets up and walks away, the boys would get up and follow her. And when the boys get up and walk away, Lady would get up and follow them as well. They are inseparable.

Lady revels in the relationship with her two new companions. She imagines things that she can do with them down the road. What she has in her mind is a picture of a happy family life. This is truly a remarkable dream-come-true for an once very lonely lioness.

"Wuh-ooow, wuh-ooow, I am not alone any more, I have two mates," proudly announces Lady, while strolling along in the field. Her announcement echoes through the vast-open-plains of Liuwa and reaches many, many ears from birds' to hyenas'.

****

Thereafter the trio starts on a journey of discovery. Lady leads her mates into the open plains to introduce them to the new way of life in the Liuwa Plain. Before the boys, there is a view of never-ending savanna in every direction. Here and there a group of flowers blooms, adding another dimension of scenic splendor to the vast savanna.

"But where are the rocks and trees?" ask the boys. The two males' old home is dotted with woodlands. They are accustomed with rocky hills and woods and are unfamiliar with grasslands. The idea of being exposed in open plains freezes them. They need rocks and trees for cover.

"For trees we can go to the fringe of the grassland, there, you will see the woodland which is interspersed with palm trees or sausage trees." Lady points to the far end.

"We rather start in the woodland to play it safe," say the males. So, they move from woodland to woodland exploring and avoid the grasslands.

During the first week, the boys wander off. Before they know it they are lost. They find themselves in the floodplain. They are amazed by the sight of huge flocks of different kinds of birds from the Grey-crowned crane to the pelican. Each lion kills a bird for his lunch. The bird meat doesn't taste bad, but feather plucking is troublesome. They also see lots of large catfishes in the limpid water. Since they have never fed on fish before, one brother dips his paw into the water to catch one. Both sniff the fish and make a grimace. Fish is definitely not on their menu.

Lady Liuwa waits patiently for the boys to come home. She understands that boys are full of adventure. *"Let the boys do what boys always do."* However, on the third day she starts to worry about them. She sets off to find her mates before anything bad happens to them.

In the mean time park rangers keep a close eye on the trio, monitoring every move (24 / 7) via the collar-signals. They are prepared to act if necessary. They see that the two males have wandered off too far into floodplains without Lady.

One of the staff calls Simon who's out in the field, *"Simon, the two males have wandered off into floodplains without Lady."*

"How long has it been?"

"Four days."

Simon slumps into his chair. *"Four days, that's too long. I'll come over now,"* says Simon.

On his way over to the AP staff office, his mind is reeling off the lion restoration program from the beginning. This program has meant a lot to him. It really started when he was a child. A child enthralled by wildlife, particularly big cats. One of his favorite pastimes, as a little boy, was going in a jeep with his dad lion-watching. But it was becoming harder and harder to spot any lion in the Liuwa Plain as he got older. His dad told him that poachers had killed the big cats. He couldn't believe it; that was too devastating for the tender heart of a young child to accept.

Later, as a grown man, he was able to accept the fact that poachers had killed the lions, but he wasn't ready to roll over and play dead. *"We must do something to right the wrong."* With a determination like this he studied zoology and worked for African Parks Network. His goal is to restock wildlife in Zambia in particular, overall in Africa.

The legendary Lady Liuwa, the last lioness in the Liuwa Plain emerged like a fairy tale with a happy ending—or is it? He felt so strong about her; he wanted so much to make her happy. But, if the two males ran off and never returned, there would not be a happing ending. Oh, God! He clutches his head at the horrible thought.

Upon arriving the site, he jumps out of his Land Cruiser and waves at the rangers. He has made up his mind to track down the two escapees right away. *"Hi, guys, we got to find them. Let's go."*

Just when the rangers are about to act, the male's collar-signal is moving closer to home, closer to Lady's collar. *"Wait a minute; I don't think we need to find them. They are coming home...."* A big relief for all; plus a wide smile on Simon's face.

The boys are back home. Lady takes them to hunt. She knows all the best hunting spots. The trio will do group hunt. Since Lady is now an experienced-stellar hunter, she plays the lead role. With their formidable joint force the trio goes after big game—matured wildebeest and zebra and, perhaps, buffalo. While the trio feeds on a kill, hyenas cautiously stand behind. Who dares to mess around with the kings and queen of Liuwa Plain!

She also teaches the males how to survive during the rainy season: Stay on high ground. During the rainy season all the ground animals congregate on pockets of high-lands. A spectrum of choices at hand; not bad for the lions. All the more, even though the prey tries to escape when chased, it is forced to run into the water and that makes an easy fetch for the lions due to the prey's mobility being constrained by water.

To the lions' delight they see more and more wildebeest and zebra herds crossing the plains. It seems that the lean time is over, and the feast is a common scene. Our little pride is enjoying the fruits of a successful, wildlife-rehabilitation program.

"Wuh-ooow, wuh-ooow— This is our land," proclaims the trio, *"our sweet, home land. We are the bravest in this land."*

One hears the trio's roar vibrating throughout the vast-open-plains against the back drop of a spectacular-golden sunset. Once again the landscape is restocked with animals, wild and free.

Lady has been mating with both males. They have formed a solid pride. Just when will we hear the pitter-patter of little paws? Time will tell. There is always tomorrow; there is always hope. History has proved that a new horizon brings a new hope.

The Epilogue

To follow up on Lady Liuwa update, please click on:
http://www.african-parks.org/
http://www.africanparks-conservation.com/

www.ingramcontent.com/pod-product-compliance
Lightning Source LLC
Chambersburg PA
CBHW060644290526
45793CB00001B/388